BIBLE FIRSTS

Math Mysteries to Solve

William Schlegl
Illustrated by Ed Koehler

3558 S. Jefferson Avenue, St. Louis, MO 63118-3968
Manufactured in the United States of America

1 2 3 4 5 6 7 8 9 10 08 07 06 05 04 03 02 01 00 99

TABLE OF CONTENTS

To Teachers and Parents:

Bible Firsts has been designed to give students of the Bible a list of "first" occurrences in the Bible.

Beginning with the "First Day" and going to the "First Christians," adolescents and adults will find the puzzles an exciting way to learn more about God's Word, the Bible. While children may have fun working together on the puzzles, adult Bible classes might find the puzzles an interesting change of pace in their lessons.

Please note that sometimes the complete reference is not used for the answer. In such cases, you will see an ellipses (...) used to indicate omitted words.

Try these challenging ways to adapt and use *Bible Firsts*:

1. Photocopy the pages without the code. Place one number or letter at a time on the chalkboard until someone completes the puzzle.
2. Make up a different code for every puzzle.
3. Look in reference books to discover other interesting facts about each "Bible First."
4. Make up your own puzzle about each "Bible First."
5. Write a newspaper story about your favorite "Bible First." Try to write an eye-catching headline.

Enthusiasm makes learning an enjoyable experience. Enjoy working on each puzzle activity!

William Schlegl

"But seek first His kingdom." (Matthew 6:33a)

FIRST DAY

Our heavenly Father is eternal, without beginning and without end. However, the world had a beginning when God created the heavens and the earth. What happened on the very first day of the world?

Solve:

A	22 + 17 = _____	B	28 + 59 = _____	C	13 + 12 = _____
D	67 + 12 = _____	E	47 + 28 = _____	F	12 + 14 = _____
G	36 + 49 = _____	H	39 + 54 = _____	I	57 + 16 = _____
K	27 + 28 = _____	L	14 + 19 = _____	M	21 + 67 = _____
N	32 + 38 = _____	O	82 + 14 = _____	R	33 + 58 = _____
S	52 + 14 = _____	T	26 + 38 = _____	V	44 + 28 = _____
W	18 + 19 = _____	Y	63 + 35 = _____		

73 70   64 93 75   87 75 85 73 70 70 73 70 85   85 96 79

25 91 75 39 64 75 79   64 93 75   93 75 39 72 75 70 66   39 70 79

64 93 75   75 39 91 64 93.   85 96 79   25 39 33 33 75 79   64 93 75

33 73 85 93 64   "79 39 98,"   39 70 79   64 93 75

79 39 91 55 70 75 66 66   93 75   25 39 33 33 75 79   "70 73 85 93 64."

39 70 79   64 93 75 91 75   37 39 66   75 72 75 70 73 70 85,

39 70 79   64 93 75 91 75   37 39 66   88 96 91 70 73 70 85

64 93 75   26 73 91 66 64   79 39 98.

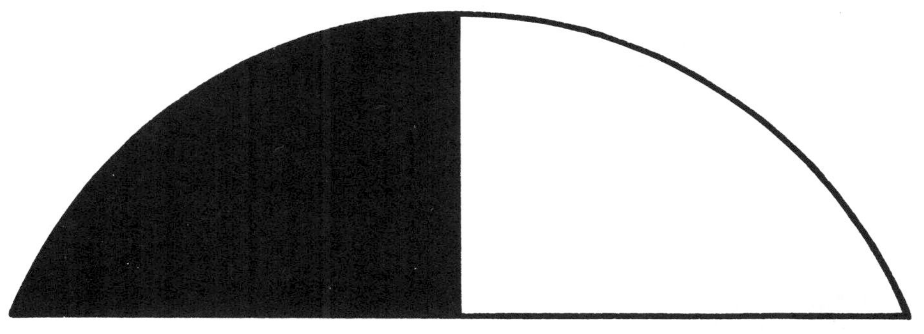

FIRST MAN

The Lord created everything in the world by saying "Let there be," and it was done. However, man was made in a completely different way. What special method did the Lord use to make the first man?

How Many...

A	V + L = _____	B	III + LVI = _____	C	IX + XII = _____
D	IX +XVII = _____	E	CC + CCC = _____	F	V + XXXVI = _____
G	XX + XXX = _____	H	XVII + VIII = _____	I	IV + VII = _____
L	XII + X = _____	M	D + D = _____	N	V + VIII = _____
O	L + L = _____	R	XIV + XVI = _____	S	VI + LV = _____
T	II + V = _____	U	LIII + XLVIII = _____	V	DC + DC = _____

VII XXV D   XXII C XXX XXVI   L C XXVI   XLI C XXX M D XXVI

VII XXV D   M LV XIII   XLI XXX C M

VII XXV D   XXVI CI LXI VII   C XLI   VII XXV D

L XXX C CI XIII XXVI   LV XIII XXVI

LIX XXX D LV VII XXV D XXVI   XI XIII VII C

XXV XI LXI   XIII C LXI VII XXX XI XXII LXI   VII XXV D

LIX XXX D LV VII XXV   C XLI   XXII XI XLI D,   LV XIII XXVI

VII XXV D   M LV XIII   LIX D XXI LV M D   LV

XXII XI MCC XI XIII L   LIX D XI XIII L.

FIRST WOMAN

After making the first man, the Lord saw that it was not good for man to be alone. What unusual way did the Lord make the first woman?

How Many ...

A Fours in two hundred forty? _____

B Fours in one hundred ninety-two? _____

D Tens in five hundred? _____

E Sixes in four hundred ninety-two? _____

F Threes in forty-eight? _____

G Threes in one hundred seventeen? _____

H Ones in ninety-eight? _____

I Nines in two hundred fifty-two? _____

K Nines in eight hundred nineteen? _____

L Sevens in one hundred five? _____

M Sevens in two hundred seventeen? _____

N Fours in eighty-eight? _____

O Threes in one hundred fifty-six? _____

R Fives in two hundred? _____

T Twos in one hundred thirty-four? _____

U Ones in twenty-five? _____

W Fives in four hundred sixty-five? _____

67 98 82 22   67 98 82   15 52 40 50   39 52 50

31 60 50 82   60   93 52 31 60 22   16 40 52 31

67 98 82   40 28 48   98 82   98 60 50   67 60 91 82 22

52 25 67   52 16   67 98 82   31 60 22'   60 22 50

98 82   48 40 52 25 39 98 67   98 82 40

67 52   67 98 82   31 60 22.

FIRST GARDEN

Pretty flowers and green shrubs in a garden make a happy and pleasant surrounding. God made a beautiful garden for Adam and Eve. Where was this garden located?

Find the product:

A	12 × 36 =	_____	D	23 × 32 =	_____	E	10 × 99 =	_____
F	28 × 16 =	_____	G	13 × 68 =	_____	H	34 × 29 =	_____
I	12 × 12 =	_____	L	27 × 36 =	_____	M	17 × 53 =	_____
N	12 × 58 =	_____	O	24 × 41 =	_____	P	13 × 14 =	_____
R	19 × 52 =	_____	S	18 × 46 =	_____	T	25 × 25 =	_____
U	37 × 15 =	_____	W	19 × 27 =	_____			

696 984 513   625 986 990   972 984 988 736   884 984 736

986 432 736   182 972 432 696 625 990 736   432

884 432 988 736 990 696   144 696   625 986 990   990 432 828 625,

144 696   990 736 990 696;   432 696 736   625 986 990 988 990

986 990   182 555 625   625 986 990   901 432 696   986 990

986 432 736   448 984 988 901 990 736.

FIRST SIN

The Lord told Adam and Eve that they were not to eat fruit from the tree of the knowledge of good and evil. The serpent deceived Eve, telling her that she would be like God, knowing good and evil, if she ate the fruit. How was the first sin committed?

Find the average for each group of numbers:

A	35, 59, 87, 67 = _____	B	98, 82, 99, 85 = _____
D	68, 41, 57, 70 = _____	E	17, 19, 42, 18 = _____
F	58, 95, 73, 58 = _____	G	15, 12, 37, 12 = _____
H	69, 82, 99, 94 = _____	I	70, 28, 93, 69 = _____
K	24, 52, 63, 17 = _____	L	28, 35, 26, 35 = _____
M	37, 33, 43, 51 = _____	N	52, 76, 62, 82 = _____
O	86, 96, 76, 54 = _____	P	21, 28, 26, 41 = _____
R	32, 65, 28, 63 = _____	S	95, 93, 91, 77 = _____
T	59, 65, 28, 72 = _____	U	38, 28, 38, 32 = _____
W	70, 68, 47, 67 = _____	Y	70, 96, 85, 57 = _____

63 86 24 68 56 86 24 63 78 41 62 68 89 62 63 56 86 62 56

56 86 24 71 47 34 65 56 78 71 56 86 24 56 47 24 24 63 62 89

19 78 78 59 71 78 47 71 78 78 59 62 68 59 29 31 24 62 89 65 68 19

56 78 56 86 24 24 77 24' 62 68 59 62 31 89 78

59 24 89 65 47 62 91 31 24 71 78 47 19 62 65 68 65 68 19

63 65 89 59 78 41' 89 86 24 56 78 78 39 89 78 41 24 62 68 59

62 56 24 65 56.

FIRST CLOTHING

Adam and Eve were both naked, but being without sin, they felt no shame. Eating the fruit of the forbidden tree brought sin into the world. How did sin affect the way Adam and Eve looked at each other?

Add 7 to each number:

A	B	C	D	E	F	G	H	I	J	K	L	M
37	51	83	46	92	17	29	58	66	31	22	55	71
N	O	P	Q	R	S	T	U	V	W	X	Y	Z
85	12	34	53	42	90	89	14	39	40	10	77	63

96 65 99 92   96 65 99   99 84 99 97   19 24   58 19 96 65

19 24   96 65 99 78   47 99 49 99   19 41 99 92 99 53,   44 92 53

96 65 99 84   49 99 44 62 73 70 99 53   96 65 99 84   47 99 49 99

92 44 29 99 53;   97 19   96 65 99 84   97 99 47 99 53   24 73 36

62 99 44 46 99 97   96 19 36 99 96 65 99 49   44 92 53   78 44 53 99

90 19 46 99 49 73 92 36 97   24 19 49

96 65 99 78 97 99 62 46 99 97.

FIRST PROMISE OF A SAVIOR

What a terrible tragedy it was when sin entered the world. All would be lost. But the Lord promised Adam and Eve He would send a Savior to redeem the world from sin. What was the first promise of a Savior?

Rename:

A	168 inches = _____ft.	B	3 feet = _____in.	C	11 yards = _____ft.
D	117 feet = _____yd.	E	2 feet = _____in.	F	4 feet = _____ in.
G	171 feet = _____yd.	H	23 yards = _____ft.	I	222 feet = _____yd.
K	228 inches = _____ft.	L	144 inches = _____ft.	M	156 feet = _____yd.
N	282 feet = _____yd.	O	5 feet = _____in.	P	2 yards = _____in.
R	14 yards = _____ft.	S	255 feet = _____yd.	T	183 feet = _____yd.
U	7 feet = _____in.	W	8 feet = _____in.	Y	31 yards = _____ft.

14 94 39   74   96 74 12 12   72 84 61   24 94 52 74 61 93

36 24 61 96 24 24 94   93 60 84   14 94 39   61 69 24

96 60 52 14 94,   14 94 39   36 24 61 96 24 24 94   93 60 84 42

60 48 48 85 72 42 74 94 57   14 94 39   69 24 42 85;   69 24

96 74 12 12   33 42 84 85 69   93 60 84 42   69 24 14 39,

14 94 39   93 60 84   96 74 12 12   85 61 42 74 19 24

69 74 85   69 24 24 12.

FIRST BIRTH

Adam and Eve were the parents of all mankind. The Bible tells us that the first birth came after Adam and Eve were sent away from the Garden of Eden. What did Eve say when she gave birth to show that she still trusted in the Lord?

Solve:

A	(9 x 9) - (6 - 4) =	_____	B	(4 x 8) - (7 + 7) =	_____
C	(3 x 9) + (3 + 2) =	_____	D	(6 x 6) + (6 + 5) =	_____
E	(2 x 8) - (8 - 5) =	_____	F	(5 x 9) - (2 + 3) =	_____
G	(4 x 6) + (9 + 9) =	_____	H	(4 x 4) + (5 + 2)=	_____
I	(5 x 8) - (7 - 2) =	_____	L	(9 x 8) - (7 + 4) =	_____
M	(7 x 7) + (9 + 8) =	_____	N	(7 x 8) + (7 - 4) =	_____
O	(4 x 3) - (7 - 6) =	_____	P	(6 x 9) - (3 + 2) =	_____
R	(7 x 6) + (8 + 7) =	_____	S	(6 x 4) - (2 + 2) =	_____
T	(4 x 5) + (9 - 1) =	_____	U	(9 x 7) - (9 - 2) =	_____
V	(6 x 8) - (3 + 7) =	_____	W	(7 x 3) + (8 - 7) =	_____
Y	(2 x 7) + (8 + 4) =	_____			

79 47 79 66 61 79 26 22 35 28 23 23 35 20 22 35 40 13

13 38 13' 79 59 47 20 23 13 18 13 32 79 66 13

49 57 13 42 59 79 59 28 79 59 47 42 79 38 13, 18 35 57 28 23

"28 11 32 79 35 59. 20 23 13 20 79 35 47' 22 35 28 23

28 23 13 23 13 61 49 11 40 28 23 13 61 11 57 47 35

23 79 38 13 18 57 11 56 42 23 28 40 11 57 28 23 79

66 79 59."

FIRST MURDER

Cain and Abel both offered sacrifices to the Lord. Abel's sacrifice was accepted while Cain's sacrifice was not. This made Cain angry. What did Cain's sinful anger cause him to do while both brothers were walking in the field?

Solve:

A	67 - 39 = ____	B	88 - 67 = ____	C	57 - 19 = ____
D	78 - 27 = ____	E	96 - 78 = ____	F	92 - 44 = ____
G	87 - 28 = ____	H	33 - 19 = ____	I	39 - 17 = ____
K	79 - 12 = ____	L	55 - 28 = ____	M	66 - 14 = ____
N	49 - 18 = ____	O	98 - 35 = ____	R	25 - 13 = ____
S	73 - 16 = ____	T	91 - 58 = ____	U	64 - 38 = ____
W	93 - 54 = ____	Y	75 - 28 = ____		

31 63 39   38 28 22 31   57 28 22 51   33 63   14 22 57

21 12 63 33 14 18 12   28 21 18 27,   “27 18 33 ’ 57   59 63

63 26 33   33 63   33 14 18   48 22 18 27 51.”   28 31 51

39 14 22 27 18   33 14 18 47   39 18 12 18   22 31

33 14 18   48 22 18 27 51,   38 28 22 31   28 33 33 28 38 67 18 51

14 22 57   21 12 63 33 14 18 12   28 21 18 27

28 31 51   67 22 27 27 18 51   14 22 52.

FIRST MAN TO WALK WITH GOD

Through sin, death entered the world. All people must die and have their bodies returned to the earth. However, Enoch was different. What happened to Enoch at the end of his life on earth?

Place each word in the slot that matches the correct time:

Him - Seven forty-three
God - Twelve fifty-nine
Was - Three fifteen
Years - Six eighteen
Then - One oh one
No - Four fifty-four
365 - Two forty-eight
Took - Five thirty-six
More - Six forty-nine
Altogether - Ten forty-one

Lived - Two thirty-five
Walked - Five twenty-seven
Enoch - Eleven forty-two
Because - Ten forty-nine
God - Nine twenty-three
Away - Seven thirty-nine
He - Twelve seventeen
Enoch - Three twenty-five
With - Eleven fifty

10:41	11:42	2:35	2:48	6:18
3:25	5:27	11:50	9:23	1:01
12:17	3:15	4:54	6:49	10:49
12:59	5:36	7:43	7:39	
				.

FIRST RAINBOW

The first rainbow was given as the sign of a promise. God made the first rainbow for Noah after the great flood. What should we be reminded of every time we see a rainbow?

Add:

A	61 + 47 + 21 + 28 =	_____	B	91 + 87 + 74 + 47 =	_____
C	68 + 92 + 12 + 43 =	_____	D	50 + 87 + 72 + 24 =	_____
E	69 +75 + 29+ 81 =	_____	F	16 + 79 + 84 + 58 =	_____
G	97 + 93 + 89 + 47 =	_____	H	65 +76 + 87 + 94 =	_____
I	67 + 56 + 39 + 74 =	_____	L	24 + 16 + 39 + 72 =	_____
M	42 + 12 + 78 + 37 =	_____	N	49 + 27 + 86 + 58 =	_____
O	61 + 76 + 92+ 49 =	_____	R	35 +21 + 47 + 87 =	_____
S	58 + 24 + 87+ 81 =	_____	T	98 + 39 + 72 + 47 =	_____
U	97 + 92 + 89 + 94 =	_____	V	58 + 62 + 36 + 23 =	_____
W	19 + 58 + 36 + 17 =	_____	Y	77 + 88 + 99 + 66 =	_____

"236 322 157 179 254 250 254 256 169 330

190 157 236 220 299 278 130 236 220 256 322 254

215 151 278 372 233 250, 157 220 233 236 256 130 236 151 151

299 254 256 322 254 250 236 326 220 278 237 256 322 254

215 278 179 254 220 157 220 256 299 254 256 130 254 254 220

169 254 157 220 233 256 322 254 254 157 190 256 322....

220 254 179 254 190 157 326 157 236 220 130 236 151 151

256 322 254 130 157 256 254 190 250 299 254 215 278 169 254

157 237 151 278 278 233 256 278 233 254 250 256 190 278 330"

157 151 151 151 236 237 254.

FIRST LANGUAGES

At first, all people in the world spoke the same language. After the great flood, people started to build a tall tower to the heavens so they could make a name for themselves. How did God stop the completion of this mighty tower?

How many ...

A	Dimes equal six dollars? ______	B	Nickels equal six quarters? ______
C	Nickels equal three quarters? ______	D	Dimes equal nine dollars? ______
E	Pennies equal three quarters? ______	F	Pennies equal seven dimes? ______
G	Quarters equal six dollars? ______	H	Quarters equal nine dollars? ______
I	Dimes equal four dollars? ______	L	Nickels equal seven quarters? ______
N	Pennies equal a half-dollar? ______	O	Pennies equal nineteen nickels? ______
R	Nickels equal a dollar? ______	S	Dimes equal eight dollars? ______
T	Dimes equal a dollar? ______	U	Quarters equal four dollars? ______
W	Pennies equal a quarter? ______	Y	Nickels equal seven dimes? ______

10 36 60 10   40 80   25 36 14   40 10   25 60 80

15 60 35 35 75 90   30 60 30 75 35

30 75 15 60 16 80 75   10 36 75 20 75   10 36 75

35 95 20 90   15 95 50 70 16 80 75 90   10 36 75

35 60 50 24 16 60 24 75   95 70   10 36 75

25 36 95 35 75   25 95 20 35 90.

FIRST PATRIARCH

God called Abraham to be the father of His chosen people. Several times the Lord repeated His message to Abraham. What was the special message given to Abraham, the first patriarch?

Find the missing number in each series:

A	17, 18, 20, 21, 22	______	B	51, 52, 53, 54, 56	______
D	47, 48, 49, 51, 52	______	E	84, 86, 87, 88, 89	______
G	75, 76, 78, 79, 80	______	I	93, 94, 95, 97, 98	______
K	28, 29, 30, 32, 33	______	L	15, 16, 17, 19, 20	______
M	63, 65, 66, 67, 68	______	N	22, 23, 25, 26, 27	______
O	44, 45, 46, 47, 49	______	R	35, 36, 37, 39, 40	______
S	67, 68, 70, 71, 72	______	T	69, 70, 72, 73, 74	______
U	79, 81, 82, 83, 84	______	W	88, 89, 90, 91, 93	______
Y	57, 58, 60, 61, 62	______			

"

96 92 96 18 18 64 19 31 85 59 48 80

96 24 71 48 19 77 38 85 19 71

24 19 71 96 48 24 19 24 50 96 92 96 18 18

55 18 85 69 69 59 48 80; 96

92 96 18 18 64 19 31 85 59 48 80 38

24 19 64 85 77 38 85 19 71,

19 24 50 59 48 80 92 96 18 18 55 85

19 55 18 85 69 69 96 24 77."

FIRST SON OF JACOB

Jacob had twelve sons. His name was later changed to Israel, and his descendants were called the children of Israel. What special honors came to Jacob's first son?

Multiply:

A	9 × 7 = _____	B	9 × 9 = _____	C	5 × 6 = _____
E	8 × 9 = _____	F	4 × 7 = _____	G	8 × 5 = _____
H	3 × 9 = _____	I	2 × 8 = _____	L	7 × 3 = _____
M	8 × 8 = _____	N	8 × 7 = _____	O	4 × 8 = _____
P	5 × 5 = _____	R	9 × 5 = _____	S	7 × 6 = _____
T	6 × 8 = _____	U	2 × 7 = _____	W	7 × 7 = _____
X	3 × 8 = _____	Y	9 × 4 = _____		

"45 72 14 81 72 56, 36 32 14 63 45 72 64 36

28 16 45 42 48 81 32 45 56, 64 36 64 16 40 27 48,

48 27 72 28 16 45 42 48 42 16 40 56

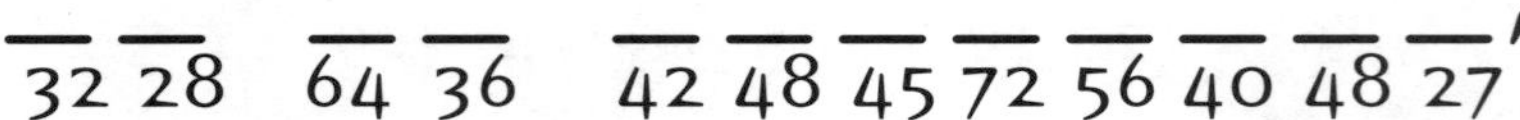

32 28 64 36 42 48 45 72 56 40 48 27,

72 24 30 72 21 21 16 56 40, 16 56

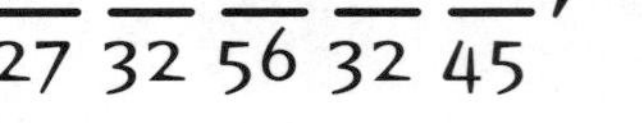

27 32 56 32 45, 72 24 30 72 21 21 16 56 40"

16 56 25 32 49 72 45.

FIRST PLAGUE

The Egyptians had many gods in nature. The ten plagues were sent to show them that the God of Israel was more powerful than all the gods of Egypt. The Nile River was one of their worldly gods. How did God show His almighty power over the Nile River?

Find the square root of each number:

A	B	C	D	E	F	G	H	I	J	K
144	529	289	729	961	841	196	625	361	576	121

L	M	N	O	P	R	S	T	U	V	W
400	256	324	169	900	676	225	784	100	441	484

16 13 15 31 15   12 18 27   12 12 26 13 18   27 19 27   24 10 15 28

12 15   28 25 31   20 13 26 27   25 12 27   17 13 16 16 12 18 27 31 27.

25 31   26 12 19 15 31 27   25 19 15   15 28 12 29 29   19 18   28 25 31

30 26 31 15 31 18 17 31   13 29   30 25 12 26 12 13 25   12 18 27

25 19 15   13 29 29 19 17 19 12 20 15   12 18 27

15 28 26 10 17 11   28 25 31   22 12 28 31 26   13 29   28 25 31

18 19 20 31'   12 18 27   12 20 20   28 25 31   22 12 28 31 26

22 12 15   17 25 12 18 14 31 27   19 18 28 13   23 20 13 13 27.

FIRST PASSOVER

As the tenth plague, the Lord passed through the entire land of Egypt, killing the firstborn in every household. However, God gave the Israelites specific directions for protection. What were the Israelites to do?

Multiply each number by 6:

A	B	C	D	E	F	G	H	I	J	K	L	M
78	42	36	53	99	27	52	88	91	57	46	24	33

N	O	P	Q	R	S	T	U	V	W	X	Y	Z
66	59	44	75	96	30	62	48	72	85	21	50	81

372 528 594   252 144 354 354 318   510 546 144 144

252 594   468   180 546 312 396   162 354 576

300 354 288   354 396   372 528 594

528 354 288 180 594 180   510 528 594 576 594   300 354 288

468 576 594;   468 396 318   510 528 594 396   546   180 594 594

372 528 594   252 144 354 354 318,   546

510 546 144 144   264 468 180 180   354 432 594 576

300 354 288.   396 354   318 594 180 372 576 288 216 372 546 432 594

264 144 468 312 288 594   510 546 144 144

372 354 288 216 528   300 354 288   510 528 594 396   546

180 372 576 546 276 594   594 312 300 264 372.

FIRST COMMANDMENT

God gave Moses the Ten Commandments as the Israelities were moving from Egypt to the Promised Land. These commandments were given as a guide to be used by God's people. Can you think of a reason why the First Commandment was given first?

Use the coordinates to solve this puzzle:

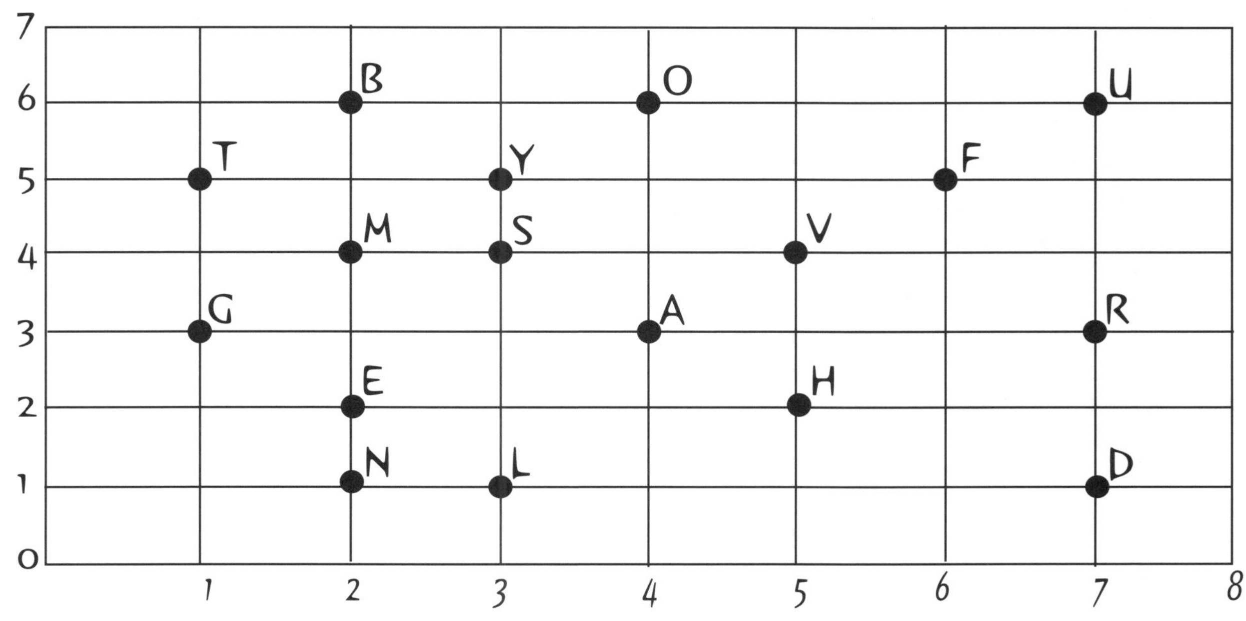

3,5 4,6 7,6   3,4 5,2 4,3 3,1 3,1

5,2 4,3 5,4 2,2   2,1 4,6   4,6 1,5 5,2 2,2 7,3

1,3 4,6 7,1 3,4   2,6 2,2 6,5 4,6 7,3 2,2

2,4 2,2.

FIRST TABERNACLE

The first tabernacle was set up to be a place of worship for the Israelites as they wandered through the wilderness. God's people brought some of their possessions to help construct the tabernacle. What special instructions did God give to Moses concerning the first tabernacle?

Solve:

A	941 - 654 = _____	B	718 - 251 = _____	C	775 - 148 = _____
D	946 - 290 = _____	E	335 - 146 = _____	F	923 - 159 = _____
G	877 - 298 = _____	H	975 - 627 = _____	I	893 - 369 = _____
L	603 - 349 = _____	M	847 - 584 = _____	N	672 - 287 = _____
O	783 - 159 = _____	P	806 - 397 = _____	R	654 - 396 = _____
S	839 - 487 = _____	T	369 - 246 = _____	U	791 - 632 = _____
Y	417 - 209 = _____				

123 348 189 385   123 348 189   254 624 258 656

352 287 524 656   123 624   263 624 352 189 352 :   "352 189 123

159 409   123 348 189   123 287 467 189 258 385 287 627 254 189 ,

123 348 189   123 189 385 123   624 764

263 189 189 123 524 385 579 ,   624 385   123 348 189

764 524 258 352 123   656 287 208   624 764

123 348 189   764 524 258 352 123

263 624 385 123 348 ."

FIRST HIGH PRIEST

The Lord selected the tribe of Levi to be priests. The priests were to lead the Israelites in worshiping God and in making sacrifices. How was the first high priest set apart from the others?

How many...

A	Days are in a week? _____	B	Inches are in a foot? _____
C	Feet are in a yard? _____	D	Days are in March? _____
E	Books are in the Bible? _____	F	Hours are in a day? _____
G	Letters are in *dictionary?*_____	H	Pennies are in a quarter? _____
I	Weeks are in a year? _____	L	Fingers are on a hand? _____
M	Quarts are in a gallon? _____	N	Inches are in a yard? _____
O	Days are in September? _____	P	Players are on a baseball team? _____
R	Letters are in *understanding?* _____	S	Minutes are in an hour? _____
T	Books are in the Old Testament? _____	U	Cups are in a pint? _____
W	Books are in the New Testament? _____		

39 25 66 36   4 30 60 66 60   12 13 30 2 10 25 39

7 7 13 30 36   7 36 31   25 52 60   60 30 36 60

24 30 13 27 7 13 31   7 36 31   27 7 60 25 66 31

39 25 66 4   27 52 39 25   27 7 39 66 13.   25 66

9 30 2 13 66 31   60 30 4 66   30 24   39 25 66

7 36 30 52 36 39 52 36 10   30 52 5   30 36   7 7 13 30 36 ' 60

25 66 7 31   7 36 31   7 36 30 52 36 39 66 31   25 52 4   39 30

3 30 36 60 66 3 13 7 39 66   25 52 4.

FIRST CENSUS

A census is a numbering or accounting of a group of people. The Lord wanted a census taken of the children of Israel after they left Egypt. How detailed was this first census?

Solve:

A	251 + 467 = ____	B	146 + 189 = ____	C	348 + 627 = ____
D	584 + 263 = ____	E	397 + 409 = ____	F	246 + 123 = ____
G	208 + 743 = ____	H	627 +148 = ____	I	159 + 764 = ____
K	369 + 524 = ____	L	385 + 287 = ____	M	396 + 258 = ____
N	632 + 159 = ____	O	256 + 321 = ____	R	654 + 287 = ____
S	290 + 656 = ____	T	349 + 254 = ____	U	487 + 352 = ____
V	579 + 298 = ____	W	624 + 159 = ____	Y	209 + 208 = ____

603 718 893 806   718   975 806 791 946 839 946   577 369

603 775 806   783 775 577 672 806

923 946 941 718 806 672 923 603 806

975 577 654 654 839 791 923 603 417   335 417

603 775 806 923 941   975 672 718 791 946   718 791 847

369 718 654 923 672 923 806 946,   672 923 946 603 923 791 951

806 877 806 941 417   654 718 791   335 417

791 718 654 806,   577 791 806   335 417   577 791 806.

FIRST JUDGE

The children of Israel were faithful to God for a while, but then became disobedient to His will. God punished Israel for their unfaithfulness, but He also sent judges as leaders to help restore His land to peace. What did the Israelites do to warrant God's sending of their first judge?

Subtract 12 from each number:

A	B	C	D	E	F	G	H	I	J	K	L	M
34	90	55	49	74	31	38	80	83	57	68	51	72
N	O	P	Q	R	S	T	U	V	W	X	Y	Z
27	78	96	70	84	63	59	45	41	24	87	52	89

78 33 47   12 68 62 15   47 68 62 40   43 72 71 62 37   66 33 47

47 66   47 68 62   39 66 72 37,   68 62   72 22 71 51 62 37

33 84   19 66 72   47 68 62 60   22   37 62 39 71 29 62 72 62 72,

66 47 68 15 71 62 39,   51 66 15   66 19   56 62 15 22 77,

43 22 39 62 78   51   40 66 33 15 26 62 72   78 72 66 47 68 62 72,

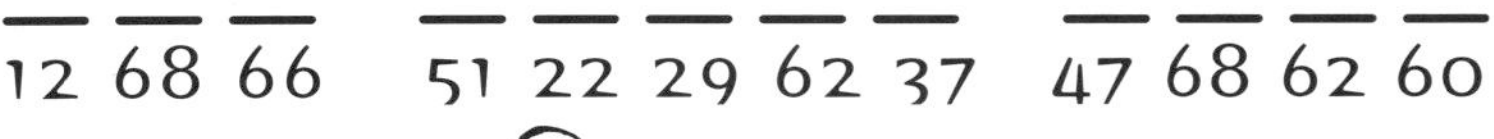

12 68 66   51 22 29 62 37   47 68 62 60.

FIRST PROPHETESS

God chose women as well as men to lead and guide the children of Israel. Deborah was a woman judge, also called a prophetess. What special task did a prophetess do?

Solve:

A	(8 × 9) - (6 × 4) = _____	B	(4 × 8) - (2 × 6) = _____	C	(7 × 6) - (4 × 2) = _____
D	(5 × 7) - (4 × 3) = _____	E	(9 × 9) - (2 × 3) = _____	F	(6 × 4) - (2 × 3) = _____
G	(7 × 8) - (4 × 5) = _____	H	(9 × 5) - (3 × 5) = _____	I	(8 × 6) - (3 × 5) = _____
L	(6 × 6) - (1 × 1) = _____	M	(8 × 8) - (2 × 2) = _____	N	(9 × 8) - (2 × 5) = _____
O	(9 × 6) - (2 × 4) = _____	P	(7 × 7) - (3 × 2) = _____	R	(6 × 7) - (3 × 6) = _____
S	(2 × 9) - (2 × 3) = _____	T	(9 × 9) - (5 × 8) = _____	U	(8 × 7) - (5 × 7) = _____
V	(7 × 9) - (2 × 5) = _____	W	(7 × 9) - (5 × 7) = _____	Y	(5 × 6) - (2 × 7) = _____

23 75 20 46 24 48 30, 48 43 24 46 43 30 75 41 75 12 12,

41 30 75 28 33 18 75 46 18 35 48 43 43 33 23 46 41 30,

28 48 12 35 75 48 23 33 62 36 33 12 24 48 75 35 48 41

41 30 48 41 41 33 60 75. 12 30 75 30 75 35 23 34 46 21 24 41

21 62 23 75 24 41 30 75 43 48 35 60 46 18

23 75 20 46 24 48 30 . . . 48 62 23 41 30 75

33 12 24 48 75 35 33 41 75 12 34 48 60 75 41 46 30 75 24

41 46 30 48 53 75 41 30 75 33 24 23 33 12 43 21 41 75 12

23 75 34 33 23 75 23.

FIRST PROPHET

A prophet was one who spoke and guided people in understanding God's Word. How did the children of Israel show that they accepted God's prophet?

Find the product:

A	3 × 179 = ____	B	2 × 458 = ____	C	3 × 321 = ____
D	7 × 123 = ____	E	5 × 193 = ____	F	2 × 341 = ____
G	4 × 176 = ____	H	2 × 123 = ____	I	6 × 108 = ____
L	3 × 246 = ____	M	6 × 142 = ____	N	3 × 198 = ____
O	4 × 206 = ____	P	9 × 109 = ____	R	2 × 486 = ____
S	5 × 125 = ____	T	3 × 298 = ____	U	4 × 178 = ____
W	7 × 119 = ____	Z	6 × 147 = ____		

537 594 861 537 738 738 648 625 972 537 965 738

682 972 824 852 861 537 594 894 824

916 965 965 972 625 246 965 916 537

972 965 963 824 704 594 648 882 965 861 894 246 537 894

625 537 852 712 965 738 833 537 625

537 894 894 965 625 894 965 861 537 625 537

981 972 824 981 246 965 894 824 682

894 246 965 738 824 972 861.

FIRST KING OF ISRAEL

The children of Israel were led by prophets and judges for many years. Then they wanted to be ruled by a king. God selected Saul to be the first king of Israel. How did the Israelites confirm Saul as their king?

Write the numeral:

A Four hundred twenty-eight _____
B Two hundred thirty-one _____
C Six hundred ninety-two _____
D One hundred fifty-three ___
E Three hundred seventy-four _____
F Five hundred eighty-seven _____
G Seven hundred fifteen _____
H Eight hundred forty-five _____
I Nine hundred ninety-nine _____
K Four hundred nineteen _____
L Two hundred sixty-two _____
M Six hundred twenty-two _____
N One hundred eighty-one _____
O Two hundred forty-four _____
P Three hundred sixty-five _____
R Five hundred ninety-seven _____
S Seven hundred sixteen _____
T Eight hundred thirty-one _____
U Six hundred nineteen _____
W Nine hundred twenty-four _____
Y Seven hundred eighty-two _____

716 244 428 262 262 831 845 374 365 374 244 365 262 374

924 374 181 831 831 244 715 999 262 715 428 262 428 181 153

692 244 181 587 999 597 622 374 153 716 428 619 262 428 716

419 999 181 715 999 181 831 845 374

365 597 374 716 374 181 692 374 244 587 831 845 374

262 244 597 153 . 831 845 374 597 374 831 845 374 782

716 428 692 597 999 587 999 692 374 153

587 374 262 262 244 924 716 845 999 365

244 587 587 374 597 999 181 715 716 231 374 587 244 597 374

831 845 374 262 244 597 153 .

FIRST TEMPLE

The temple was to be a permanent building for worship. It would replace the moveable tabernacle used previously by the Israelites. How many years had elapsed since the children of Israel had come out of Egypt before the start of the new temple?

Add

A	3 + 7 + 8 + 4 = _____	B	9 + 8 + 9 + 8 = _____
C	4 + 4 + 3 + 5 = _____	D	2 + 3 + 3 + 2 = _____
E	2 + 5 + 7 + 3 = _____	F	6 + 5 + 6 + 9 = _____
G	6 + 1 + 2 + 3 = _____	H	8 + 7 + 8 + 8 = _____
I	9 + 9 + 9 + 9 = _____	L	3 + 4 + 3 + 4 = _____
M	4 + 5 + 9 + 2 = _____	N	5 + 9 + 8 + 7 = _____
O	3 + 6 + 8 + 7 = _____	P	9 + 9 + 8 + 9 = _____
R	9 + 8 + 7 + 6 = _____	S	8 + 9 + 8 + 8 = _____
T	6 + 7 + 6 + 8 = _____	U	6 + 7 + 2 + 8 = _____
V	8 + 9 + 1 + 1 = _____	Y	3 + 3 + 4 + 5 = _____

36 29   27 31 17   26 24 23 30   31 23 29 10 30 17 10   22 29 10

17 36 12 31 27 36 17 27 31   15 17 22 30   22 26 27 17 30   27 31 17

36 33 30 22 17 14 36 27 17 33   31 22 10   16 24 20 17   24 23 27

24 26   17 12 15 35 27 ’   36 29   27 31 17   26 24 23 30 27 31

15 17 22 30   24 26   33 24 14 24 20 24 29 ’ 33   30 17 36 12 29

24 19 17 30   36 33 30 22 17 14 …   31 17   34 17 12 22 29

27 24   34 23 36 14 10   27 31 17   27 17 20 35 14 17   24 26

27 31 17   14 24 30 10.

FIRST KING OF JUDAH

Sin caused many changes in the world. The land of Israel was divided into two countries, Israel and Judah. Why did the first king of Judah have his capital in Jerusalem?

Divide each number by 7:

A	B	C	D	E	F	G	H	I	J	K	L	M
238	399	595	434	105	539	273	301	693	133	182	336	147

N	O	P	Q	R	S	T	U	V	W	X	Y	Z
546	651	462	623	378	315	672	504	119	413	567	441	196

54 15 43 93 57 93 34 21   45 93 78   93 77   45 93 48 93 21 93 78

59 34 45   26 99 78 39   99 78   19 72 62 34 43.   43 15

59 34 45   77 93 54 96 63 - 93 78 15   63 15 34 54 45   93 48 62

59 43 15 78   43 15   57 15 85 34 21 15

26 99 78 39,   34 78 62   43 15   54 15 99 39 78 15 62

45 15 17 15 78 96 15 15 78   63 15 34 54 45   99 78

19 15 54 72 45 34 48 15 21,   96 43 15

85 99 96 63   96 43 15   48 93 54 62   43 34 62

85 43 93 45 15 78   93 72 96   93 77   34 48 48   96 43 15

96 54 99 57 15 45   93 77   99 45 54 34 15 48   99 78

59 43 99 85 43   96 93   66 72 96   43 99 45   78 34 21 15.

FIRST RAISING FROM THE DEAD

Elijah was a prophet. He stayed with the widow of Zarephath and her son. One day the widow's son died. What strange way did Elijah pray to God to raise the boy from the dead?

Change all answers to lowest terms:

A	95/96 - 11/96 =	______	B	22/72 + 38/72 =	______
C	32/48 - 14/48 =	______	D	24/80 + 40/80 =	______
E	3/8 × 4/12 =	______	F	44/55 - 11/55 =	______
G	31/56 + 17/56 =	______	H	16/65 + 10/65 =	______
I	13/63 + 32/63 =	______	L	28/60 - 16/60 =	______
M	4/6 × 6/7 =	______	N	22/72 + 32/72 =	______
O	3/4 × 4/7 =	______	R	4/8 × 6/12 =	______
S	14/98 + 14/98 =	______	T	12/42 + 16/42 =	______
U	3/7 × 3/9 =	______	Y	35/69 - 12/69 =	______

2/3 2/5 1/8 3/4   2/5 1/8   2/7 2/3 1/4 1/8 2/3 3/8 2/5 1/8 4/5

2/5 5/7 4/7 2/7 1/8 1/5 3/5   3/7 1/7 2/3   3/7 3/4

2/3 2/5 1/8   5/6 3/7 1/3   2/3 2/5 1/4 1/8 1/8

2/3 5/7 4/7 1/8 2/7   7/8 3/4 4/5   3/8 1/4 5/7 1/8 4/5

2/3 3/7   2/3 2/5 1/8   1/5 3/7 1/4 4/5,   "3/7

1/5 3/7 1/4 4/5   4/7 1/3   6/7 3/7 4/5,   1/5 1/8 2/3

2/3 2/5 5/7 2/7   5/6 3/7 1/3 ' 2/7   1/5 5/7 3/5 1/8

1/4 1/8 2/3 1/7 1/4 3/4   2/3 3/7   2/5 5/7 4/7."

FIRST PURIM

The word "pur" was originally used for the day when the Jews were to be totally destroyed. Yet the Jews have a reason to celebrate Purim every year with happiness instead of sadness. What happened to make Purim a happy occasion?

Multiply:

A	6 × 87 = _____	B	3 × 56 = _____	C	9 × 23 = _____
D	3 × 47 = _____	E	2 × 83 = _____	F	4 × 59 = _____
G	8 × 35 = _____	H	7 × 62 = _____	I	3 × 98 = _____
J	6 × 72 = _____	L	2 × 96 = _____	M	7 × 49 = _____
N	5 × 55 = _____	O	7 × 43 = _____	P	8 × 87 = _____
R	3 × 74 = _____	S	6 × 57 = _____	T	2 × 76 = _____
U	6 × 93 = _____	W	8 × 22 = _____	Y	9 × 19 = _____

152 434 166 342 166   141 522 171 342   176 166 222 166

207 522 192 192 166 141   696 558 222 294 343'   236 222 301 343

152 434 166   176 301 222 141   696 558 222 . . .   522 342

152 434 166   152 294 343 166   176 434 166 275   152 434 166

432 166 176 342   280 301 152   222 166 192 294 166 236

236 222 301 343   152 434 166 294 222   166 275 166 343 294 166 342'

522 275 141   522 342   152 434 166   343 301 275 152 434

176 434 166 275   152 434 166 294 222   342 301 222 222 301 176

176 522 342   152 558 222 275 166 141   294 275 152 301

432 301 171   522 275 141   152 434 166 294 222

343 301 558 222 275 294 275 280   294 275 152 301   522

141 522 171   301 236   207 166 192 166 168 222 522 152 294 301 275.

FIRST CHRISTMAS

The first promise of a Savior was fulfilled in the little town of Bethlehem on the first Christmas. Jesus, the Savior, was born in a stable alongside cows, goats, and other animals. Why was Jesus born in such lowly surroundings?

Solve:

A	(987 - 254) + 156 =	______	B	(29 × 32) - 189 =	______
C	(198 + 147) + 345 =	______	D	661 - (25 × 16) =	______
E	807 - (19 × 28) =	______	F	(358 + 247) + 159 =	______
G	(746 - 367) + 365 =	______	H	(36 × 24) - 369 =	______
I	129 + (459 + 321) =	______	L	254 + (147 + 214) =	______
M	(27 × 36) - 102 =	______	N	(23 × 14) - 158 =	______
O	(254 + 369) - 358 =	______	P	972 - (32 × 15) =	______
R	347 + (32 × 19) =	______	S	(326 + 428) - 254 =	______
T	(17 × 26) - 126 =	______	U	(999 - 358) + 282 =	______
V	124 + (325 + 258) =	______	W	127 + (145 + 187) =	______

889 164 261 500 495 275 744 889 707 275

739 909 955 316 495 316 265 495 275 955

764 909 955 500 316 739 265 955 164, 889

500 265 164. 500 495 275 459 955 889 492 492 275 261

495 909 870 909 164 690 615 265 316 495 500

889 164 261 492 615 889 690 275 261 495 909 870

909 164 889 870 889 164 744 275 955,

739 275 690 889 923 500 275 316 495 275 955 275 459 889 500

164 265 955 265 265 870 764 265 955 316 495 275 870

909 164 316 495 275 909 164 164.

FIRST DISCIPLES

Jesus chose disciples to follow Him in His ministry on earth. Many of Jesus' disciples were fishermen. The fish they caught in their nets were sold at the marketplace. What did Jesus tell His first disciples that they would now catch instead of fish?

A	32 + 47 = _____	B	56 + 19 = _____	C	26 + 27 = _____
D	65 + 12 = _____	E	55 + 44 = _____	F	18 + 27 = _____
G	13 + 14 = _____	H	28 + 36 = _____	I	47 + 39 = _____
J	24 + 37 = _____	K	69 + 14 = _____	L	11+ 12 = _____
M	27 + 38 = _____	N	15 + 17 = _____	O	32 + 34 = _____
P	25 + 24 = _____	R	63 + 28 = _____	S	36 + 49 = _____
T	34 + 47 = _____	U	15 + 10 = _____	W	37 + 37 = _____
Y	10 + 19 = _____				

79 85   61 99 85 25 85   74 79 85   74 79 23 83 86 32 27

75 99 85 86 77 99   81 64 99   85 99 79   66 45

27 79 23 86 23 99 99'   64 99   85 79 74   81 74 66

75 91 66 81 64 99 91 85'   85 86 65 66 32   53 79 23 23 99 77

49 99 81 99 91   79 32 77   64 86 85   75 91 66 81 64 99 91

79 32 77 91 99 74 ....   81 64 99 29   74 99 91 99

45 86 85 64 99 91 65 99 32.   "53 66 65 99'   45 66 23 23 66 74

65 99"   61 99 85 25 85   85 79 86 77'   "79 32 77   86

74 86 23 23   65 79 83 99   29 66 25   45 86 85 64 99 91 85

66 45   65 99 32."

FIRST MIRACLE OF JESUS

Jesus performed many miracles while on earth. His first miracle was changing water into wine at the wedding in Cana. What special purpose did Jesus have for performing His first miracle?

How many ...

A Days are in a week? _____
D Eyes are on 7 eagles? _____
F Pennies equal a nickel? _____
H Trunks are on an elephant? _____
J Wheels are on 8 bicycles? _____
M Toes are on 2 feet? _____
O Paws are on 2 kittens? _____
R Feet equal one yard? _____
T Donuts are in a dozen? _____
V Months are in 2 years? _____

C Noses are on 11 horses? _____
E Wheels are on 3 tricycles? _____
G Legs are on 9 ducks? _____
I Ears are on 2 dogs? _____
L Tails are on 13 cows? _____
N Fingers are on 3 hands? _____
P Wings are on a bird? _____
S Legs are on 3 chickens? _____
U Days are in 3 weeks? _____
Y Minutes are in an hour? _____

12 1 4 6,   12 1 9   5 4 3 6 12   8 5   1 4 6

10 4 3 7 11 21 13 8 21 6   6 4 18 15 6,   16 9 6 21 6

2 9 3 5 8 3 10 9 14   4 15   11 7 15 7   8 5

18 7 13 4 13 9 9.   1 9   12 1 21 6   3 9 24 9 7 13 9 14

1 4 6   18 13 8 3 60,   7 15 14   1 4 6

14 4 6 11 4 2 13 9 6   2 21 12   12 1 9 4 3

5 7 4 12 1   4 15   1 4 10.

FIRST PALM SUNDAY

This special day occurred at the beginning of Holy Week, one week before the first Easter. Jesus came to the city of Jerusalem to sacrifice Himself for us. Why do we call this Sunday "Palm Sunday"?

If A = 1, E = 5, I = 9, O = 15, U = 21, then...

20 8 5   14 5 24 20   4 1 25   20 8 5   7 18 5 1 20

3 18 15 23 4   20 8 1 20   8 1 4   3 15 13 5   6 15 18

20 8 5   6 5 1 19 20   8 5 1 18 4   20 8 1 20

10 5 19 21 19   23 1 19   15 14   8 9 19   23 1 25

20 15   10 5 18 21 19 1 12 5 13.   20 8 5 25   20 15 15 11

16 1 12 13   2 18 1 14 3 8 5 19   1 14 4   23 5 14 20

15 21 20   20 15   13 5 5 20   8 9 13,

19 8 15 21 20 9 14 7,   "8 15 19 1 14 14 1!"

"2 12 5 19 19 5 4   9 19   8 5   23 8 15

3 15 13 5 19   9 14   20 8 5   14 1 13 5

15 6   20 8 5   12 15 18 4!"   "2 12 5 19 19 5 4

9 19   20 8 5   11 9 14 7   15 6

9 19 18 1 5 12!"

FIRST LORD'S SUPPER

The first Lord's Supper was celebrated the night before Jesus was crucified. We call this day Maundy Thursday. What blessing did Jesus say we receive when we partake of His Body and Blood through the Lord's Supper?

Add 12 to each number.

A	B	C	D	E	F	G	H	I	J	K	L	M
34	58	72	14	87	65	79	10	27	31	82	22	54
N	**O**	**P**	**Q**	**R**	**S**	**T**	**U**	**V**	**W**	**X**	**Y**	**Z**
37	51	25	84	39	20	15	76	61	19	56	28	13

43 99 32 88 32   27 63 63 94   70 51 99 46 26, . . . "27 46 94 99"

46 49 26   99 46 27;   27 22 39 32   39 32   66 40   70 63 26 40.

27 22 99 49   22 99   27 63 63 94   27 22 99   84 88 37, . . .

"26 51 39 49 94   77 51 63 66   39 27,   46 34 34   63 77

40 63 88.   27 22 39 32   39 32   66 40   70 34 63 63 26

63 77   27 22 99   84 63 73 99 49 46 49 27,   31 22 39 84 22

39 32   37 63 88 51 99 26   63 88 27   77 63 51   66 46 49 40

77 63 51   27 22 99   77 63 51 91 39 73 99 49 99 32 32   63 77

32 39 49 32."

FIRST GOOD FRIDAY

Good Friday is sometimes called the darkest day in the history of the world. It was on that day that the Son of God died for the sins of all people. Where was Jesus crucified?

____

Multiply:

A 32 × 24 = ____	B 12 × 36 = ____	C 42 × 11 = ____
D 18 × 35 = ____	E 28 × 13 = ____	F 52 × 11 = ____
G 27 × 26 = ____	H 29 × 31 = ____	I 14 × 17 = ____
J 56 × 14 = ____	K 24 × 21 = ____	L 91 × 10 = ____
M 35 × 17 = ____	N 31 × 18 = ____	O 19 × 17 = ____
P 25 × 25 = ____	R 28 × 21 = ____	S 33 × 30 = ____
T 48 × 11 = ____	U 33 × 23 = ____	W 49 × 20 = ____
Y 10 × 10 = ____		

528 899 364 100 432 588 323 759 702 899 528

784 364 990 759 990 528 323 528 899 364 625 910 768 462 364

462 768 910 910 364 630 702 323 910 702 323 528 899 768

(980 899 238 462 899 595 364 768 558 990

528 899 364 625 910 768 462 364 323 572 528 899 364

990 504 759 910 910). 238 528 980 768 990

528 899 364 528 899 238 588 630 899 323 759 588

980 899 364 558 528 899 364 100

462 588 759 462 238 572 238 364 630

899 238 595.

FIRST EASTER

Wonderful words were spoken by an angel at the empty tomb on the first Easter morning. The women who came to the grave could not find Jesus' body. What wonderful news did the angel tell the women?

Subtract:

A 86 - 34 = _____	B 98 - 32 = _____	C 58 - 36 = _____
D 65 - 28 = _____	E 99 - 10 = _____	F 91 - 32 = _____
G 84 - 35 = _____	H 85 - 68 = _____	I 91 - 14 = _____
J 80 - 24 = _____	K 55 - 27 = _____	L 89 - 57 = _____
M 93 - 49 = _____	N 90 - 29 = _____	O 79 - 54 = _____
P 77 - 38 = _____	R 96 - 85 = _____	S 77 - 26 = _____
T 86 - 39 = _____	U 97 - 77 = _____	W 83 - 68 = _____
Y 94 - 12 = _____		

47 17 89   52 61 49 89 32   51 52 77 37   47 25   47 17 89

15 25 44 89 61,   “37 25   61 25 47   66 89   52 59 11 52 77 37,

59 25 11   77   28 61 25 15   47 17 52 47   82 25 20   52 11 89

32 25 25 28 77 61 49   59 25 11   56 89 51 20 51,   15 17 25   15 52 51

22 11 20 22 77 59 77 89 37.   17 89   77 51   61 25 47   17 89 11 89;

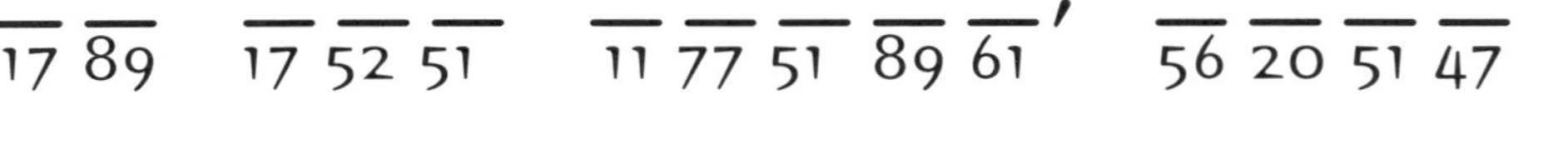

17 89   17 52 51   11 77 51 89 61,   56 20 51 47

52 51   17 89   51 52 77 37.   22 25 44 89   52 61 37

51 89 89   47 17 89   39 32 52 22 89”

15 17 89 11 89   17 89   32 52 82.

FIRST RESURRECTION APPEARANCE

"He is not here. He has risen!" the angel said. What great joy these words bring to all Christians. Jesus appeared to a woman on the first Easter morning. How had He previously helped this woman?

Find the average for each group of numbers:

A	25, 17, 59, 51 = _____	D	69, 53, 47, 43 = _____	E	89, 48, 86, 53 = _____
F	99, 90, 98, 93 = _____	G	34, 19, 37, 22 = _____	H	25, 27, 29, 91 = _____
I	12, 18, 19, 19 = _____	J	47, 19, 38, 24 = _____	K	73, 28, 86, 49 = _____
L	68, 63, 87, 90 = _____	M	50, 70, 55, 65 = _____	N	12, 19, 14, 15 = _____
O	17, 34, 23, 18 = _____	P	38, 65, 42, 51 = _____	R	32, 39, 31, 42 = _____
S	84, 99, 96, 85 = _____	T	78, 68, 76, 66 = _____	U	76, 92, 81, 83 = _____
V	39, 35, 36, 74 = _____	W	20, 30, 20, 30 = _____	Y	56, 93, 42, 65 = _____

25 43 69 15   32 69 91 83 91   36 23 91 69   69 38 36 77 64

23 15   72 43 69   95 17 36 91 72   53 38 64   23 95   72 43 69

25 69 69 59'   43 69   38 49 49 69 38 36 69 53   95 17 36 91 72

72 23   60 38 36 64   60 38 28 53 38 77 69 15 69'   23 83 72

23 95   25 43 23 60   43 69   43 38 53   53 36 17 46 69 15

91 69 46 69 15   53 69 60 23 15 91.

FIRST PENTECOST

Pentecost was also called the Feast of Harvest or the Gathering of the Crops. Something spectacular happened on the first Pentecost. What special ability was given to the disciples to help them preach the Good News of salvation to all people?

If A = 26, E = 22, I = 18, O = 12, U = 6, then...

8 6 23 23 22 13 15 2   26   8 12 6 13 23   15 18 16 22   7 19 22

25 15 12 4 18 13 20   12 21   26   5 18 12 15 22 13 7

4 18 13 23   24 26 14 22   21 9 12 14   19 22 26 5 22 13   26 13 23

21 18 15 15 22 23   7 19 22   4 19 12 15 22   19 12 6 8 22

4 19 22 9 22   7 19 22 2   4 22 9 22   8 18 7 7 18 13 20.

7 19 22 2   8 26 4   4 19 26 7   8 22 22 14 22 23   7 12

25 22   7 12 13 20 6 22 8   12 21   21 18 9 22   7 19 26 7

8 22 11 26 9 26 7 22 23   26 13 23   24 26 14 22   7 12

9 22 8 7   12 13   22 26 24 19   12 21   7 19 22 14.

26 15 15   12 21   7 19 22 14   4 22 9 22   21 18 15 15 22 23

4 18 7 19   7 19 22   19 12 15 2   8 11 18 9 18 7   26 13 23

25 22 20 26 13   7 12   8 11 22 26 16   18 13   12 7 19 22 9

7 12 13 20 6 22 8   26 8   7 19 22   8 11 18 9 18 7

22 13 26 25 15 22 23   7 19 22 14.

FIRST CHRISTIAN MARTYR

A martyr is someone who chooses to die rather than renounce or deny religious beliefs. Stephen, the first Christian martyr, spoke to the Lord before he died. What unusual request did Stephen ask of the Lord?

Divide each number by 6:

A	B	C	D	E	F	G	H	I	J	K	L	M
342	432	246	492	396	462	306	414	312	366	594	522	324

N	O	P	Q	R	S	T	U	V	W	X	Y	Z
450	282	510	546	276	576	228	360	354	468	204	258	540

78 69 52 87 66   38 69 66 43   78 66 46 66   96 38 47 75 52 75 51

69 52 54,   96 38 66 85 69 66 75   85 46 57 43 66 82

“87 47 46 82   61 66 96 60 96,   46 66 41 66 52 59 66   54 43

96 85 52 46 52 38.”   38 69 66 75   69 66   77 66 87 87

47 75   69 52 96   99 75 66 66 96   57 75 82   41 46 52 66 82

47 60 38,   “87 47 46 82,   82 47   75 47 38   69 47 87 82

38 69 52 96   96 52 75   57 51 57 52 75 96 38   38 69 66 54.”

78 69 66 75   69 66   69 57 82   96 57 52 82   38 69 52 96,

69 66   77 66 87 87   57 96 87 66 66 85.

FIRST CALLED CHRISTIANS

A Christian is one who follows the teachings of Jesus Christ. Early believers used to be called "Followers of the Way." Where were the followers of Jesus first called "Christians"?

Find the sum:

A 74 + 36 +98 + 47 = _____

B 28 + 96 + 74 + 28 = _____

C 63 + 69 + 61 + 65 = _____

D 81 + 36 + 74 + 25 = _____

E 78 + 96 + 56 + 73 = _____

F 85 + 69 + 78 + 87= _____

G 26 + 27 + 29 + 28 = _____

H 27 + 96 + 37 + 42 = _____

I 59 + 67 + 58 + 76 = _____

L 58 + 85 + 34 + 57 = _____

M 53 + 48 + 69 + 87 = _____

N 98 + 87+ 76 + 92 = _____

O 94 + 87 + 96 + 99 = _____

P 12 + 57 + 39 + 68= _____

R 83 + 57 + 53 + 78 = _____

S 71 + 63 + 98 + 14 = _____

T 47 + 65 + 59 + 74 = _____

U 45 + 36 + 57 + 68 = _____

W 74 + 35 + 59 + 96 = _____

Y 79 + 95 + 68 + 99 = _____

246 376   319 376 271   255   264 202 376 234 303

341 303 255 271   226 255 271 353 255 226 255 246

255 353 216   246 255 206 234   257 303 245

264 260 245 202   245 202 303   258 202 206 271 258 202

255 353 216   245 255 206 110 202 245   110 271 303 255 245

353 206 257 226 303 271 246   376 319   176 303 376 176 234 303.

245 202 303   216 260 246 258 260 176 234 303 246

264 303 271 303   258 255 234 234 303 216

258 202 271 260 246 245 260 255 353 246

319 260 271 246 245   255 245   255 353 245 260 376 258 202.

ANSWER KEY

First Day . . . .(5)

A=39, B=87, C=25, D=79, E=75, F=26, G=85, H=93, I=73, K=55, L=33, M=88, N=70, O=96, R=91, S=66, T=64, V=72, W=37, Y=98.

In the beginning God created the heavens and the earth. God called the light "day," and the darkness He called "night." And there was evening, and there was morning—the first day. (Genesis 1:1, 5)

First Man . . . .(6)

A=LV, B=LIX, C=XXI, D=XXVI, E=D, F=XLI, G=L, H=XXV, I=XI, L=XXII, M=M, N=XIII, O=C, R=XXX, S=LXI, T=VII, U=CI, V=MCC.

The LORD God formed the man from the dust of the ground and breathed into his nostrils the breath of life, and the man became a living being. (Genesis 2:7)

First Woman . . . .(7)

A=60, B=48, D=50, E=82, F=16, G=39, H=98, I=28, K=91, L=15, M=31, N=22, O=52, R=40, T=67, U=25, W=93.

Then the LORD God made a woman from the rib He had taken out of the man, and He brought her to the man. (Genesis 2:22)

First Garden . . . .(8)

A=432, D=736, E=990, F=448, G=884, H=986, I=144, L=972, M=901, N=696, O=984, P=182, R=988, S=828, T=625, U=555, W=513.

Now the LORD God had planted a garden in the east, in Eden; and there He put the man He had formed. (Genesis 2:8)

First Sin . . . .(9)

A=62, B=91, D=59, E=24, F=71, G=19, H=86, I=65, K=39, L=31, M=41, N=68, O=78, P=29, R=47, S=89, T=56, U=34, W=63, Y=77.

When the woman saw that the fruit of the tree was good for food and pleasing to the eye, and also desirable for gaining wisdom, she took some and ate it. (Genesis 3:6)

First Clothing . . . .(10)

A=44, B=58, C=90, D=53, E=99, F=24, G=36, H=65, I=73, J=38, K=29, L=62, M=78, N=92, O=19, P=41, Q=60, R=49, S=97, T=96, U=21, V=46, W=47, X=17, Y=84, Z=70.

Then the eyes of both of them were opened, and they realized they were naked; so they sewed fig leaves together and made coverings for themselves. (Genesis 3:7)

First Promise of a Savior . . . .(11)

A=14, B=36, C=33, D=39, E=24, F=48, G=57, H=69, I=74, K=19, L=12, M=52, N=94, O=60, P=72, R=42, S=85, T=61, U=84, W=96, Y=93.

And I will put enmity between you and the woman, and between your offspring and hers; he will crush your head, and you will strike his heel. (Genesis 3:15)

First Birth . . . .(12)

A=79, B=18, C=32, D=47, E=13, F=40, G=42, H=23, I=35, L=61, M=66, N=59, O=11, P=49, R=57, S=20, T=28, U=56, V=38, W=22, Y=26.

Adam lay with his wife Eve, and she became pregnant and gave birth to Cain. She said, "With the help of the LORD I have brought forth a man." (Genesis 4:1)

First Murder . . . .(13)

A=28, B=21, C=38, D=51, E=18, F=48, G=59, H=14, I=22, K=67, L=27, M=52, N=31, O=63, R=12, S=57, T=33, U=26, W=39, Y=47.

Now Cain said to his brother Abel, "Let's go out to

the field." And while they were in the field, Cain attacked his brother Abel and killed him. (Genesis 4:8)

First Man to Walk with God . .(14)

Him=7:43, Lived=2:35, God=12:59, Walked=5:27, Was=3:15, Enoch=11:42, Years=6:18, Because=10:49, Then=1:01, God=9:23, No=4:54, Away=7:39, 365=2:48, He=12:17, Took=5:36, Enoch=3:25, More=6:49, With=11:50, Altogether=10:41.

Altogether, Enoch lived 365 years. Enoch walked with God; then he was no more, because God took him away. (Genesis 5:23–24)

First Rainbow . . . .(15)

A=157, B=299, C=215, D=233, E=254, F=237, G=326, H=322, I=236, L=151, M=169, N=220, O=278, R=190, S=250, T=256, U=372, V=179, W=130, Y=330.

"I have set My rainbow in the clouds, and it will be the sign of the covenant between Me and the earth. ... Never again will the waters become a flood to destroy all life." (Genesis 9:13, 15)

First Languages . . . .(16)

A=60, B=30, C=15, D=90, E=75, F=70, G=24, H=36, I=40, L=35, N=50, O=95, R=20, S=80, T=10, U=16, W=25, Y=14.

That is why it was called Babel—because there the LORD confused the language of the whole world. (Genesis 11:9)

First Patriarch . . . .(17)

A=19, B=55, D=50, E=85, G=77, I=96, K=31, L=18, M=64, N=24, O=48, R=38, S=69, T=71, U=80, W=92, Y=59.

"I will make you into a great nation and I will bless you; I will make your name great, and you will be a blessing." (Genesis 12:2)

First Son of Jacob . . . .(18)

A=63, B=81, C=30, E=72, F=28, G=40, H=27, I=16, L=21, M=64, N=56, O=32, P=25, R=45, S=42, T=48, U=14, W=49, X=24, Y=36.

"Reuben, you are my firstborn, my might, the first sign of my strength, excelling in honor, excelling in power." (Genesis 49:3)

First Plague . . . .(19)

A=12, B=23, C=17, D=27, E=31, F=29, G=14, H=25, I=19, J=24, K=11, L=20, M=16, N=18, O=13, P=30, R=26, S=15, T=28, U=10, V=21, W=22.

Moses and Aaron did just as the LORD had commanded. He raised his staff in the presence of Pharaoh and his officials and struck the water of the Nile, and all the water was changed into blood. (Exodus 7:20)

First Passover . . . .(20)

A=468, B=252, C=216, D=318, E=594, F=162, G=312, H=528, I=546, J=342, K=276, L=144, M=198, N=396, O=354, P=264, Q=450, R=576, S=180, T=372, U=288, V=432, W=510, X=126, Y=300, Z=486.

The blood will be a sign for you on the houses where you are; and when I see the blood, I will pass over you. No destructive plague will touch you when I strike Egypt. (Exodus 12:13)

First Commandment . . . .(21)

You shall have no other Gods before Me. (Exodus 20:3)

First Tabernacle . . . .(22)

A=287, B=467, C=627, D=656, E=189, F=764, G=579, H=348, I=524, L=254, M=263, N=385, O=624, P=409, R=258, S=352, T=123, U=159, Y=208.

Then the LORD said to Moses: "Set up the tabernacle, the Tent of Meeting, on the first day of the first month." (Exodus 40:1–2)

First High Priest . . . .(23)

A=7, B=12, C=3, D=31, E=66, F=24, G=10, H=25,

I=52, L=5, M=4, N=36, O=30, P=9, R=13, S=60, T=39, U=2, W=27.

Then Moses brought Aaron and his sons forward and washed them with water. He poured some of the anointing oil on Aaron's head and anointed him to consecrate him. (Leviticus 8:6, 12)

First Census . . . .(24)

A=718, B=335, C=975, D=847, E=806, F=369, G=951, H=775, I=923, K=893, L=672, M=654, N=791, O=577, R=941, S=946, T=603, U=839, V=877, W=783, Y=417.

Take a census of the whole Israelite community by their clans and families, listing every man by name, one by one. (Numbers 1:2)

First Judge . . . .(25)

A=22, B=78, C=43, D=37, E=62, F=19, G=26, H=68, I=71, J=45, K=56, L=39, M=60, N=15, O=66, P=84, Q=58, R=72, S=51, T=47, U=33, V=29, W=12, X=75, Y=40, Z=77.

But when they cried out to the LORD, He raised up for them a deliverer, Othniel, son of Kenaz, Caleb's younger brother, who saved them. (Judges 3:9)

First Prophetess . . . .(26)

A=48, B=20, C=34, D=23, E=75, F=18, G=36, H=30, I=33, L=35, M=60, N=62, O=46, P=43, R=24, S=12, T=41, U=21, V=53, W=28, Y=16.

Deborah, a prophetess, the wife of Lappidoth, was leading Israel at that time. She held court under the palm of Deborah … and the Israelites came to her to have their disputes decided. (Judges 4:4–5)

First Prophet . . . .(27)

A=537, B=916, C=963, D=861, E=965, F=682, G=704, H=246, I=648, L=738, M=852, N=594, O=824, P=981, R=972, S=625, T=894, U=712, W=833, Z=882.

And all Israel from Dan to Beersheba recognized that Samuel was attested as a prophet of the LORD. (1 Samuel 3:20)

First King of Israel . . . .(28)

A=428, B=231, C=692, D=153, E=374, F=587, G=715, H=845, I=999, K=419, L=262, M=622, N=181, O=244, P=365, R=597, S=716, T=831, U=619, W=924, Y=782.

So all the people went to Gilgal and confirmed Saul as king in the presence of the LORD. There they sacrificed fellowship offerings before the LORD. (1 Samuel 11:15)

First Temple . . . .(29)

A=22, B=34, C=16, D=10, E=17, F=26, G=12, H=31, I=36, L=14, M=20, N=29, O=24, P=35, R=30, S=33, T=27, U=23, V=19, Y=15.

In the four hundred and eightieth year after the Israelites had come out of Egypt, in the fourth year of Solomon's reign over Israel … he began to build the temple of the LORD. (1 Kings 6:1)

First King of Judah . . . .(30)

A=34, B=57, C=85, D=62, E=15, F=77, G=39, H=43, I=99, J=19, K=26, L=48, M=21, N=78, O=93, P=66, Q=89, R=54, S=45, T=96, U=72, V=17, W=59, X=81, Y=63, Z=28.

Rehoboam son of Solomon was king in Judah. He was forty-one years old when he became king, and he reigned seventeen years in Jerusalem, the city the LORD had chosen out of all the tribes of Israel in which to put His Name. (1 Kings 14:21)

First Raising from the Dead . .(31)

A=7/8, B=5/6, C=3/8, D=4/5, E=1/8, F=3/5, G=6/7, H=2/5, I=5/7, L=1/5, M=4/7, N=3/4, O=3/7, R=1/4, S=2/7, T=2/3, U=1/7, Y=1/3.

Then he stretched himself out on the boy three times and cried to the LORD, "O LORD my God, let this boy's life return to him." (1 Kings 17:21)

First Purim . . . .(32)

A=522, B=168, C=207, D=141, E=166, F=236, G=280, H=434, I=294, J=432, L=192, M=343, N=275, O=301, P=696, R=222, S=342, T=152,

U=558, W=176, Y=171.
(These days were called Purim, from the word *pur)* … as the time when the Jews got relief from their enemies, and as the month when their sorrow was turned into joy and their mourning into a day of celebration. (Esther 9:26a, 22a)

First Christmas . . . .(33)

A=889, B=739, C=690, D=261, E=275, F=764, G=744, H=495, I=909, L=615, M=870, N=164, O=265, P=492, R=955, S=500, T=316, U=923, V=707, W=459.
And she gave birth to her firstborn, a son. She wrapped Him in cloths and placed Him in a manger, because there was no room for them in the inn. (Luke 2:7)

First Disciples . . . .(34)

A=79, B=75, C=53, D=77, E=99, F=45, G=27, H=64, I=86, J=61, K=83, L=23, M=65, N=32, O=66, P=49, R=91, S=85, T=81, U=25, W=74, Y=29.
As Jesus was walking beside the Sea of Galilee, He saw two brothers, Simon called Peter and his brother Andrew. … They were fishermen. "Come, follow Me," Jesus said, "and I will make you fishers of men." (Matthew 4:18–19)

First Miracle of Jesus . . . . . .(35)

A=7, C=11, D=14, E=9, F=5, G=18, H=1, I=4, J=16, L=13, M=10, N=15, O=8, P=2, R=3, S=6, T=12, U=21, V=24, Y=60.
This, the first of His miraculous signs, Jesus performed in Cana of Galilee. He thus revealed His glory, and His disciples put their faith in Him. (John 2:11)

First Palm Sunday . . . .(36)

The next day the great crowd that had come for the Feast heard that Jesus was on His way to Jerusalem. They took palm branches and went out to meet Him, shouting, "Hosanna!" "Blessed is He who comes in the name of the Lord!" "Blessed is the King of Israel!" (John 12:12–13)

First Lord's Supper . . . .(37)

A=46, B=70, C-84, D=26, E=99, F=77, G=91, H=22, I=39, J=43, K=94, L=34, M=66, N=49, O=63, P=37, Q=96, R=51, S=32, T=27, U=88, V=73, W=31, X=68, Y=40, Z=25.
Jesus took bread, … "Take and eat; this is My body." Then He took the cup, … "Drink from it, all of you. This is My blood of the covenant, which is poured out for many for the forgiveness of sins." (Matthew 26: 26–28)

First Good Friday . . . .(38)

A=768, B=432, C=462, D=630, E=364, F=572, G=702, H=899, I=238, J=784, K=504, L=910, M=595, N=558, O=323, P=625, R=588, S=990, T=528, U=759, W=980, Y=100.
They brought Jesus to the place called Golgotha (which means The Place of the Skull). It was the third hour when they crucified Him.
(Mark 15:22, 25)

First Easter . . . .(39)

A=52, B=66, C=22, D=37, E=89, F=59, G=49, H=17, I=77, J=56, K=28, L=32, M=44, N=61, O=25, P=39, R=11, S=51, T=47, U=20, W=15, Y=82.
The angel said to the women, "Do not be afraid, for I know that you are looking for Jesus, who was crucified. He is not here; He has risen, just as He said. Come and see the place where He lay." (Matthew 28:5–6)

First Resurrection Appearance (40)

A=38, D=53, E=69, F=95, G=28, H=43, I=17, J=32, K=59, L=77, M=60, N=15, O=23, P=49, R=36, S=91, T=72, U=83, V=46, W=25, Y=64.
When Jesus rose early on the first day of the week, He appeared first to Mary Magdalene, out of whom He had driven seven demons. (Mark 16:9)

First Pentecost . . . .(41)

Suddenly a sound like the blowing of a violent wind came from heaven and filled the whole house where they were sitting. They saw what seemed to be tongues of fire that separated and came to rest on each of them. All of them were filled with the Holy Spirit and began to speak in other tongues as the Spirit enabled them. (Acts 2:2–4)

First Christian Martyr . . . . . .(42)

A=57, B=72, C=41, D=82, E=66, F=77, G=51, H=69, I=52, J=61, K=99, L=87, M=54, N=75, O=47, P=85, Q=91, R=46, S=96, T=38, U=60, V=59, W=78, X=34, Y=43, Z=90.

While they were stoning him, Stephen prayed, "Lord Jesus, receive my spirit." Then he fell on his knees and cried out, "Lord, do not hold this sin against them." When he had said this, he fell asleep. (Acts 7:59–60)

First Called Christians . . . . . .(43)

A=255, B=226, C=258, D=216, E=303, F=319, G=110, H=202, I=260, L=234, M=257, N=353, O=376, P=176, R=271, S=246, T=245, U=206, W=264, Y=341.

So for a whole year Barnabas and Saul met with the church and taught great numbers of people. The disciples were called Christians first at Antioch. (Acts 11:26)